GEORDIE ENGLISH

Abson Books London
First published December 2001
12th impression January 2012
Cover design Chris Bird
Image reproduced by kind
permission of Scottish Courage Ltd.

Printed by Gutenberg Press, Malta
ISBN 9 780902 920842

GEORDIE ENGLISH

compiled by Percy Douglas

ABSON
BOOKS
LONDON

5 Sidney Square London E1 2EY
Tel 020 7790 4737 Fax 020 7790 7346
email absonbooks@aol.com

PREFACE

Geordie, spoken on the banks of the River Tyne in the county of Northumberland, is one of the oldest, most distinctive and easily recognisable dialects in the British Isles. At one time it was rare to hear Geordie elsewhere in the country, but TV programmes such as *The Likely Lads, When the Boat Comes In* and *Byker Grove* have brought this rich dialect to our ears. Footballers such as Bobby and Jackie Charlton, Paul Gascoigne and Alan Shearer, and youth celebrities such as Ant and Dec and Donna Air have brought Geordie kudos to popular culture.

This is probably the best-constructed English regional dialect, with its distinctive pronunciation, its own vocabulary and a non-standard grammar. It also remains the best-preserved English regional dialect because of geographical isolation. Many present-day features of the Geordie tongue were prevalent in the different English dialects spoken throughout the land before they were eradicated when the English language was standardised during the 18th century. Then, as now, the county of Northumberland was the farthest place in England from the centre of standardisation, London; there are parts of Scotland that lie further south. Despite the 19th century industrialisation of this previously rural country, subsequent immigration has made little impact.

Nevertheless, like other dialects, there are subtle differences in speech across the region. The further you travel from the River Tyne, the softer the dialect becomes. Indeed, before the western boundary of Northumberland has been reached, the local sounds are almost Cumbrian; and in the colliery villages they speak a distinctive variety of Geordie where terms used in mining have entered everyday speech in a version known as "Pitmatic", just to complicate things further.

Hopefully, this small volume will help a greater understanding of a fine people and their speech.

Percy Douglas

CONTENTS

A

aadfashint	old-fashioned
aah	I, e.g. *aah will*
aakwad	awkward
aal	(i) all
	(ii) I will
aan	own, e.g. *mi aan hoose*
aback	behind, e.g. *privy's aback the hoose*
abbut	yes but, e.g. *abbut aal not let ye*
afeard	afraid
ahaad	hold, e.g. *aal get ahaad ov it*
amany	several
an aal	also
aneath	underneath
aside of	next to

at	(i) that, e.g. *them at's gan*
	(ii) for, e.g. *what ye stannin there at?*
	(iii) in, e.g. *aam at the hoose*
atween	between

B

baal	football
babby	infant
backeend	autumn
back-gannin	getting worse
back-ower	return, e.g. *he came back-ower tiv us*
bad	sick (sometimes badly)
badly off	poor
bairn	young child
bait	snack

battered	tired
beastie	small animal
beck	stream
beggar	fellow, e.g. *whaas the little beggar noo?*
bested	beaten (oddly, it means 'worsted')
berrer-end	majority
bi	by (when in front of a consonant, e.g. *his bi hissel*)
bide	endure, stand, e.g. *aah canna bide yon chap*
bin	been, e.g. *hoo ye bin the day?*
binno	by this time
bit	(i) small, short (ii) a short time
biv	by (when in front of a vowel, e.g. *better biv a mile*)

blate	shy, awkward
blythe	glad
bonny	(i) good-looking
	(ii) pleasant disposition
	(ii) used to exaggerate the opposite of good, e.g. *thaas made a bonny mess*
	(iv) greeting, e.g. *hoo ye bin, bonny lad?*
booza	public house
bramma	perfect
brockle	frail, precarious, uncertain
Broon	Newcastle Brown Ale, the basic diet of the Geordie
by	next to, near to. Used together with other words, originally down the pit: e.g. *inby* = inside, *upby* = up the street, *ootby* = outside, *donby* = down the street

C

cadge	beg, borrow
canna	can not
canny	good, gentle, kind, likeable and the ultimate Geordie compliment: e.g. *thaas a canny lass*. Also used to mean 'careful' and 'steady'.
caps	finishes, e.g. *that caps that*. Originally meant it could not be improved upon
cas	because
childer	children
claarty	muddy
claver	gossip
cockle	spit
cod	trick, deceive
cowee-handed	awkward
crabby	bad-tempered
crack	gossip

crackin	excellent
cuddy	stupid

D

daft	silly (sometimes daft-like)
dinna	do not, e.g. *dinna do that*
div	do (when in front of a vowel or a mute 'h', e.g. *div aah not?*)
divvent	don't
dott'n aboot	lounging
draas	trousers (literally 'drawers')
duds	working-clothes (predates the American phrase)
dump	cigarette-end

E

ee	eye
een	eyes
else	already

F

faather	father
faddy	over-particular, especially with food
fashion	(i) resemble, e.g. *he fashions his father*
	(ii) make, e.g. *aal fashion a good un*
fettle	(i) repair, e.g. *aal fettle it*
	(ii) health, mood, e.g. *aam in fine fettle*
	(iii) stop, sort out, e.g. *aal fettle him*
fly	crafty
fower	four
fretish	cold

G

ga	gave (when in front of a consonant, e.g. *ye ga tiv him!*)
gaffer	boss, foreman, supervisor
galloway	horse
gan	gone
gan arn	go ahead
gannin	going, moving, e.g. *gannin along the Scotswood Road*
gassin	talk persistently, gossip
gate	speed
gav	gave (when in front of a vowel, e.g. *he gav it us*)
geen	given, e.g. *aah would geen owt ta seen it*
geet	really

Geordie	(i) inhabitant of Tyneside
	(ii) dialect spoken on Tyneside
gi	give (when in front of a consonant)
gis	give me (when in front of a vowel)
giv	see gis
giyen	given, e.g. *he's giyen ower much*
gobby	talkative
gowk	(i) foolish
	(ii) apple core
greet	very
guess	understand (predates the American phrase)

H

haad	grasp, hold, e.g. *take haad on it*
hadaway!	(i) you don't say!
	(ii) I don't believe you
	(iii) go away
hanker	hesitate
hereaway	nearby
hevyee	have you?
him	he (but used as nominative singular, e.g. *him an me's gannin*)
hinny	canny, when referring to women, girls and children
his	he's
hod	hold, e.g. *take hod on it*
hoo	how, e.g. *hoo ye bin the day?*
hoose	house

| **howay** | come on (originally shouted when the pit cage was being lowered below ground; nowadays a shout of support for Newcastle United Football Club) |
| **hoy** | throw |

I

ingannin	go in
ist	(i) is it?, e.g. is*t fower o'clock?*
	(ii) it is, e.g. *aye ist*
iv	in (when in front of a vowel)

J

jaa	talk
jannock	fair, honest, genuine
jarra	Jarrow

jort	jerk	
jye	crooked	

K

keek	peep, pry	
kelter	condition	
ken	(i) know (knowledge)	
	(ii) be acquainted with	
	(iii) remember	

L

lad	(i) sweetheart (masculine)	
	(ii) brother	
lads	friends (not necessarily young men)	
lang	tall	

lass	(i) sweetheart (feminine)	
	(ii) wife	
lay	stop, e.g. lay *yer braggin*	
leetnin	dawn	
load	large quantity	

M

maisey	confused	
man	(i) husband, e.g. *her man*	
	(ii) must, e.g. *aah man away noo*	
	(iii) just added to the end of a sentence, e.g. *yor aal reet man*	
mangst	among	
manny	young man	

marra	friend, especially workmate (sometimes shortened to 'mar')
me	(i) I (used instead of 'I' when it forms the compound subject of a sentence, e.g. *me and her's faalen oot.* When 'me' is emphasised it is pronounced 'meah', e.g. *it wasna meah*)
mind	(i) be sure
	(ii) beware
	(iii) remember
	(iv) intention, e.g. *aav a mind ter*
	(v) just added to the end of a sentence, e.g. *he's a good lad mind*
minded	intention, e.g. *aam minded ter*
morn	tomorrow
mun	must

N

na	no (also added to the end of other words to imply negatives, e.g. *henna* = have not, *winna* = will not, *canna* = cannot
nar	near
nee	haven't any
netty	toilet
noo	now
nor	than
nowt	nothing
Nucassel	Newcastle

o

off	(i) by
	(ii) from, e.g. *borrad a tenner off him*
on	(i) of, e.g. *what are ye feared on?*
	(ii) busy, e.g. *he's on threshin'*
on't	on it e.g. *look at the legs on't*
or	than, e.g. *rather you or me*
outed	become common knowledge
ower	too, e.g. *he's ower small fer't pit*
owt	anything
owt mair?	anything else?

P

peel off	get rid of
pelt	hurry along
pet	term of endearment used by both sexes to the other
play	out of work, sick from work, e.g. *aas been playin' me fer a week*
pollis	police

Q

quick	alert

R

randy	quarrelsome
round the doors	nearby

S

safe	sure, certain
sarra	serve, e.g. *did yer sarra yer time i' the yards?*
scabby	shabby
scarry	easily frightened
scrunch	squeeze
seed	saw
seet	sight
sel	self, e.g. *his aan sel*. Often added to other words, e.g. *missel* = myself, *thosel* = yourself, *hissel* = his self
set	cause, e.g. *yaal set the roof down,* which was a cautionary remark in the pit
sharp	(i) early (ii) cold weather
Sheels	North Shields

shift	(i) shirt
	(ii) move
	(iii) working hours
shy	(i) unwilling
	(ii) short change
side	put in order
sitha!	look!
skemp	short change
skran	food
slack	not enough, e.g. *trade's slack*
snadgee	swede (vegetable)
step	walk
stewmer	tearaway

T

tab	cigarette
tackle	take on, e.g. *aal tackle that job*
tally	count
tatie	potato
teem	pour
teemin'	raining heavily
ter	to
thaas	you have
that	so, e.g. *it were that dark!*
the	frequently added to other words, e.g. the *noo* = now, *the day* = today, *the neet* = tonight, *the morn* = tomorrow
think on	remember
thor	(i) their
	(ii) they are

thumpin'	large
ti	to (when in front of a consonant, e.g. *aal gannin ti toon*)
tiv	to (when in front of a vowel, e.g. *aal gannin tiv aar hoose*)
toon	town, Newcastle (more precisely its football team, e.g. *Toon Army*)
towsher	scruffy

U

up a heyt	up in the air
us	(i) me
	(ii) we

V

varra	very

W

wadden	would not
wants	need, e.g. *aah wants a job*
war!	look out!
whey	(i) then, e.g. *wi gannin whey?*
	(ii) well, e.g. *whey aam gannin*
whey aye	definitely, e.g. *whey eye aam gannin*
whisht!	be quiet!
whyeye	yes
wi	(i) us
	(ii) with (when in front of a consonant, e.g. *gannin wi me*)
	(iii) will

winnet	will not
wor	our
worsels	ourselves

ya	you
yammer	talk incessantly
ye	you
ye bugger mar	an all-purpose expression that covers surprise, astonishment and pleasure
yer	you
yous	you (plural)

PRONUNCIATION

The basic features of the spoken Geordie are the cadence of its speech, the quirky tone and the questioning lilt at the end of each sentence.

- Outstanding in the dialect's pronunciation is the letter 'r', or 'burr' sounded from the tonsils in whatever part of the word the letter occurs. The letter 'a' is a big help. If 'r' is an initial letter, 'a' is added to the start of the word, e.g:

rain	**arrain**
roar	**arroar**

If 'r' is a middle letter, then 'a' is stressed in front of it, e.g:

early	**arly**
terrier	**tarrier**

- These are not the only instances of 'a's intrusiveness, e.g:

along	**alang**
amongst	**amangst**

Sometimes at the start of a word:

all	**aal**
old	**aad**

Sometimes at the end of a word:

blow	**blaa**
draw	**draa**

- Other letters can also intrude. One is the letter 'y', which replaces vowels, diphthongs or doubles, e.g:

pale	**pyel**
give	**gyev**
home	**hyem**
again	**agyen**
chain	**chyen**
school	**skyul**

boot	**byut**
cook	**cyuk**

Sometimes 'o' alone can intrude:

dare	**dore**
her	**hor**
bird	**bord**
earth	**orth**

While 'oo' has no difficulty, e.g:

out	**oot**
about	**aboot**
down	**doon**
strange	**stroonge**

Neither has 'ee, e.g:

great	**greet**
head	**heed**
sight	**seet**
do	**dee**

• The letter 'w' often appears suddenly in the middle of a word, e.g:

roll	**rowl**
hold	**howld**

• Diphthongs are popular (e.g. 'master' becomes '**maister**'), yet they can easily be ignored (see the previous page).

• The letter 'b' is sometimes dropped before 'e' or 'le', although occasionally 'b' is substituted for a 'v', e.g:

humble	**hummel**
timber	**timmer**
rivet	**ribet**

• Be careful when letters suddenly change places – both ways, e.g:
  'd' to 'th' ('fodder' to '**fother**')
  'th' to 'd' ('smithy' to '**smiddy**')

GRAMMAR

The structure of Geordie sentences contains some features that are common to other dialects, but many are unique to Geordie.

- Geordie is a fully-fledged dialect, definitely not a lazy language. The word 'the' is seldom shortened to ''t', it is spoken lightly, in full, and is often placed unexpectedly in front of other words (see glossary).

- Geordie contains certain verbs that are absent from Standard English, e.g. '**gan**', '**div**' and '**wi**' (*see glossary*). Some words are never used in Geordie - 'may' becomes '**can**' or '**might**', while 'shall' becomes '**will**' (except in the first person question, e.g. *shall I have a look?*).

- Certain Geordie words are a constant reminder of past English, e.g:

'those' becomes '**them**'
'which' becomes '**what**'
'because' becomes '**being as**'
'in order to' becomes '**for to**'

- Negatives are where regional dialects are most expressive and Geordie is no exception, with a definite grammar of its own, e.g:
  (i) 'impossible' means 'can't', but is changed to 'mustn't' (pronounced '**musna**')
  (ii) 'forbidden' means 'mustn't', but is changed to 'haven't got to' (pronounced '**hevna got ta**')
  (iii) 'unnecessary' means 'haven't got to', but is changed to 'don't have to' (pronounced '**dinna hev ta**')

Normally, the word 'never' is used to mean 'not under any circumstances', but the Geordie dialect uses it to say things like 'I never went to the match'. And, of course, there is the omnipresent double-negative such as 'I wouldn't have none of it'

- Questions are another area where Geordie has its own sentence construction, e.g:
  (i) 'You're not ready are you?' becomes '**You're not ready aren't you?**'
  (ii) 'You're ready aren't you?' becomes '**You're ready are you?**'

- Finally, there are other grammatical constructions illustrative of Geordie, e.g:
  (i) The personal pronoun is repeated at the end of the sentence, *e.g. ya young monkey ya*
  (ii) The subject is placed at the end of the sentence, *e.g. they've won agyen the lads*
  (iii) The third person is misplaced, *e.g. me and me marra*

School teachers have been trying to eradicate that last phrase for more than a century!

PUBLIC SPEAKING

Now you are ready for a few Geordie phrases. Here are some important ones to listen out for:

HowabottbyenaBroon?	It's your round
Eendoonlukkin	The bingo is about to start
Shutyorgob	Please keep quiet
Yegotnehyemteganti?	Please leave
Heyahardmi?	Didn't you catch my previous remark?

Why not try these interesting phrases on the locals?

Whatfettletheday?	How are you?
Nowtbutcanny	Very well, thank you
Letshowaydoonthabooza	Allow me to take you for a drink
Broonsaalroond	Drinks on me
Mindyorkiddin!	I don't believe you

OTHER TITLES AVAILABLE

Language Glossaries

American English/English American
Australian English/English Australian
Irish English/English Irish
Gay Slang
Geordie English
Lancashire English
Rhyming Cockney Slang
Scouse English
Yiddish English/English Yiddish
Scottish English/English Scottish
Yorkshire English
Home Counties English
Playground Slang
Prison Slang
Hip Hop English
Rude Rhyming Slang
Military Slang

Cumbrian English
West Country English
London Taxi Driver Slang
Police Slang

History

The Death of Kings - A history of how
the Kings & Queens of England died

Who's Buried Where? - Discover where Royalty
the famous & infamous are buried

Literary Quiz & Puzzle Books

Jane Austen   Gilbert & Sullivan
Brontë Sisters   Thomas Hardy
Charles Dickens   Sherlock Holmes
                     Shakespeare